ELECTRICIANS ON THE JOB

BY HEIDI AYARBE

MOMENTUM

Published by The Child's World®
1980 Lookout Drive • Mankato, MN 56003-1705
800-599-READ • www.childsworld.com

Content Consultant: Alcuin Raeker, Electrical
Construction Instructor, St. Cloud Technical and
Community College (SCTCC)

Photographs ©: Shutterstock Images, cover,
1, 10, 21, 23; Dmitry Kalinovsky/Shutterstock
Images, 5; iStockphoto, 6, 8, 12, 15, 17, 20, 24,
27; monkeybusinessimages/iStockphoto, 9;
Dragan Smiljkovic/iStockphoto, 11; Office for
Emergency Management. War Production Board.
1/1942-11/3/1945/National Archives and Records
Administration, 14; Kritsana Noisakul/Shutterstock
Images, 18; Aerovista Luchtfotografie/Shutterstock
Images, 28

ISBN 9781503835511
LCCN 2019943069

Printed in the United States of America

CONTENTS

MOMENTUM

FAST FACTS

What's the Job?

► Electricians work with electricity. They install and maintain the wiring needed to bring electrical power from place to place.

► All electricians have to go through an **apprenticeship**.

► Electricians work in manufacturing, in homes, office buildings, airports, stadiums, and more. They lay cable for all telecommunications, which includes telephones, computers, and internet services. They work at power plants, on transportation systems—such as subways—and more. Wherever anything uses electricity, an electrician is needed.

Important Stats

► In 2018, there were around 655,840 electricians in the United States.

► By 2026, the number of electrician jobs is expected to grow 9 percent.

► The average yearly salary for electricians in 2018 was $59,190.

Electricians are always at risk for getting burned, ► shocked, or even electrocuted. Safety is one of the most important parts of the job.

CHAPTER ONE

BECOMING AN ELECTRICIAN

Feathery white clouds drifted across the blue sky. The sun beat down on Nicholas's neck and back while sweat stung his eyes. Sunlight glinted off the river water. A large metal bridge loomed over a wide stretch of river. It would raise up for cargo ships to pass underneath, then lower back down to allow trains to pass. It needed to work smoothly so ships and trains could transport what they carried. But that day, the bridge wasn't working properly. Because of that, the train was two hours behind schedule.

Nicholas was an apprentice. He was working with an experienced **journey worker**. They had special equipment to locate a **circuit** and detect if it was on or off, tools to cut and strip wires, safety gloves and hard hats to wear, and more. Nicholas felt ready to tackle his first major assignment.

◄ Electricians can work in many different locations and in different types of weather.

▲ **The Cape Cod Canal Railroad Bridge in Massachusetts lifts for passing boats and lowers for trains.**

He talked to the bridge operator first. Electricians need all the information they can get to understand a problem. The previous day, the operator had raised the bridge several more times than normal because of heavy boat traffic. He saw smoke and heard alarms go off, but the bridge worked fine. Today, the sensors read that the bridge was not in the locked position when it closed. He couldn't risk letting the train pass with this issue. It could be dangerous.

Nicholas and the journey worker talked about how the electrical system worked in the bridge and possible problems.

▲ **Trade schools help prepare people to become electricians.**

They looked through the electrical system. There were signs it had overheated, which probably affected the sensors. They tested the circuits and discovered the damaged sensor. Then, they replaced it.

Finally, Nicholas nodded to the bridge operator. The bridge began to lower. Once it reached ground level, it locked into place with a deafening clank. The sensor lights flashed, signaling the bridge was in the locked position. It was safe to pass.

Nicholas exhaled with relief. The air filled with the scent of fuel. The train inched forward and began to pick up speed.

▲ **Apprenticeships are important in helping people learn new skills.**

Nicholas watched the train as it passed over the river and out of sight. The repair was a success.

Nicholas thought about the last handful of years. Some electricians go to a two-year college. Nicholas had decided to jump right into an apprenticeship. He had studied hard for the apprenticeship test. It lasted 2.5 hours, and there was a lot of math. After Nicholas passed the test, he had to wait for an apprenticeship to open up. While waiting, he took a math class, an electrical basics and tools class, and a class on electrical circuits and systems. Eventually, he was accepted into an apprenticeship. This program can take four or five years to finish.

▲ **Becoming a master electrician is the next step after reaching journey worker status.**

When they start out, apprentices might make 40 percent of what a journey worker makes. Each year, they receive a raise until they finish their apprentice program. Apprentice electricians are put to work right away and begin to study under a journey worker. They learn on the job.

After 8,000 hours, when apprentices finish their class work and on-the-job training, they take an exam. Once they pass the exam, they can become a journey worker. This allows them to be hired for work by a company or even work on their own. That was what Nicholas was working hard to achieve. After his success with the bridge, his dream felt closer than ever.

CHAPTER TWO

WOMEN IN THE TRADE

Jane took a big breath before walking into a California aircraft plant. It was the 1940s. She pulled her hair in a tight ponytail and straightened her striped work top. The only thing people talked about was World War II (1939–1945) and the millions of men who had left home to fight. After Jane saw a colorful Rosie the Riveter poster hanging up at the local soda shop, she began training to do electrical work. The poster encouraged women to work in jobs that men had left behind. Jane was excited to help.

Before World War II, it was rare for women to work in trade jobs. People believed these jobs were meant for men. Decades have passed since World War II, but there are still many false ideas about what kinds of jobs are good for women and men. In 2018, only around two out of 100 electricians were women.

◀ **Fewer women work in trade jobs compared with men.**

▲ **Rosie the Riveter became a well-known image of working women during World War II.**

Hannah Cooper is a female electrician. She grew up around trade jobs. She saw men pouring grey concrete to lay foundations for buildings. She also saw men laying pipes for plumbing.

▲ **Electricians sometimes work in cramped spaces.**

Men were everywhere in the trade job professions, but so
was Cooper's mom. Her mom was one of Los Angeles' first
female electricians.

Cooper didn't want to be an electrician at first. After high
school, she didn't know what she wanted to do. Cooper worked
odd jobs, saved money, and traveled. While traveling, she
realized that many of the young people she met worked in
construction. Cooper started thinking about her mom's work and
decided to go to trade school to become an electrician. Cooper
had many qualities electricians need.

Cooper was in good shape. Electricians have to be in good shape because they have a physical job. One day, they might be climbing power poles. Another day, they might be wiggling in a small space to get to an electrical box. They are often on their feet all day long. Cooper was also good at math. Electricians need this skill because much of their work depends on calculations. She also loved solving problems by running tests and using the results to figure out issues. Many electricians also like to see how things work.

Cooper was at the top of her trade school class. She became a journey worker in 2013. Cooper hoped that one day being a female electrician would not be unique. Being an electrician is a great job for anybody.

Electricians need to know how to read ▶ blueprints in order to complete projects.

CHAPTER THREE

NO TYPICAL DAY

Zack's breath came out in white puffs. Icy snow crunched under his work boots. Everything surrounding him was covered in a thick coat of ice. The night before, an ice storm downed power lines all over the city. Even the hospital, police station, and fire station were affected.

Icicles hung from power lines like tear-drop-shaped holiday lights. The high winds had created something called galloping power lines. The ice on the lines created a kind of wing, so when the winds picked up, the lines swayed and collided. This caused a power outage.

Zack strapped on his tool belt and harness. He climbed a utility pole 50 feet (15.2 m) into the air. Zack looked from the frozen lines to the **transformer**. For electricity to reach people's homes, it sometimes has to travel hundreds of miles through power lines.

◄ **Some electricians work on systems high in the air, which can be dangerous.**

▲ **Damaged power lines can take days to fix.**

The transformers on the poles push power long distances. When the lines collide, their **currents** can cause fuses and circuit breakers to blow, causing power to go off.

 The night before, transformers all over the city had been affected by the storm. Zack had a long day of work ahead of him. He led the power line emergency repair crew. When studying to be an electrician, there are many different routes people can take. For example, people can become residential, commercial, industrial, or maintenance electricians. Or, like Zack, someone might choose to become a utility electrician.

▲ **Utility electricians have to be prepared
for all types of weather conditions.**

Utility electricians specialize in working with power lines.
They work with high **voltage**. Utility electricians are called any
time of day or night, especially when there are emergencies.
Zack and his team had even been called to do jobs out of state.

Zack didn't have too many great weather days on his job. He was used to working in bad weather conditions at any time of the day.

Electricians work all over the country and on a lot of different projects. For example, Carlos worked at an amusement park overnight. Every night was different because most things in the amusement park required electricity. Some nights he would repair circuits on certain rides. Other nights he would check the electrical systems of a ride's cars.

Carlos spent most of his shift working on the amusement park's fastest roller coaster. He did an inspection of the electric motor. Each ride had to be checked every night to make sure it was working right. This is called preventative maintenance. Every detail mattered because the safety of other people was on the line.

The next day, the park was filled with people. The smell of popcorn drifted through the air. People stood in long lines to wait for their turns on the rides. The roller coaster cars lurched forward. With each click, the cars carrying excited riders climbed higher on the track. The cars reached the peak of the track and then slid quickly down.

At the end of the ride, people got off the roller coaster with big smiles on their faces. Carlos had done his job well, and the ride ran smoothly.

▲ Amusement park rides need to be
maintained so they are safe.

CHAPTER FOUR

ELECTRICITY EVERYWHERE

Thousands of **solar panels** glimmered in the Nevada desert sunrise. They surrounded a glowing tower. The tower could store solar energy day and night. From a distance, the panels looked like an alien spaceship on a lonely stretch of highway. Michael took a long drink of coffee and watched the sun's orange rays creep across the desert ground. He looked at the field of solar panels and thought about how they collected energy from the sun.

The cool morning breeze dried the sweat on his forehead. He had just finished a shift. Michael had worked all night to maintain the solar panels system at Crescent Dunes. He made sure that all of the solar panels and high-voltage equipment were connected to the power supply. Some nights he had to test wiring, equipment, and fixtures. Every night was different.

◄ **Nevada is ranked higher than most other states in its use of solar energy.**

Crescent Dunes could power as many as 75,000 homes using solar energy. Because the tower could store this energy, the sun didn't even need to be shining for the energy to be used. This new technology was exciting for the future of **renewable energy** and for electricians who specialized in solar electricity.

Electricians work in different renewable energy jobs. In California, Carmen arrived at her job for the day. She met with her crew before dawn to get their assignment. Then, they drove to their work site. The truck bumped down a dusty road. The first rays of sunlight stretched across the fields. When they arrived at their destination, a farm, Carmen shaded her eyes and looked up at a massive wind **turbine** before her.

It wasn't a farm that raised corn or wheat—it was a wind farm. Turbines rose 200 feet (61 m) above Carmen. She worked her way up the ladder and climbed into a hub at the top that housed all of the electrical gear. She had to test the electrical components and replace any that weren't working correctly. Carmen worked quickly because it was typically windier in the afternoon. High winds would make work more dangerous and difficult. When she finished, she returned to the truck and felt satisfied with her work.

Wind turbines need to be maintained ▶ in order to work properly.

▲ Wind turbines can be put on farmland.

For many years people have been getting their electrical power from things such as coal, natural gas, and nuclear plants. Now, using renewable energy sources to make electricity is a growing trend in the United States and around the world. There are many specialties for electricians in renewable energy. The future is bright for electricians.

THINK ABOUT IT

▶ Why are trade jobs important in everyday life?
▶ What would life be like with limited or no electricity?
▶ What everyday challenges do you think female electricians like Hannah Cooper face?

GLOSSARY

apprenticeship (uh-PREN-tis-ship): An apprenticeship is a type of supervised work where someone learns trade skills. To become an electrician, a person needs to complete an apprenticeship in order to gain experience through on-the-job work.

circuit (SUR-kit): A circuit is a path for electrical currents. The electrician checked the circuit.

currents (KUR-uhntz): Currents are the flow of electricity. The power line's currents caused issues and the power went off.

journey worker (JUR-nee WUR-kur): A journey worker is a person who has learned a trade and is an experienced worker. Cooper passed an exam and became a journey worker.

renewable energy (ri-NOO-uh-buhl EN-ur-jee): Renewable energy is a type of power source that can't be used up. Sources of renewable energy include solar, wind, and water.

solar panels (SOH-lur PAN-uhls): Solar panels are types of equipment that capture the sun's heat or light to make electricity. Some homes have solar panels.

transformer (trans-FOR-mur): A transformer increases or decreases an electric current's voltage. The transformer was affected by the snowstorm.

turbine (TUR-byne): A turbine is an engine that gets power from gas, steam, water, or wind passing over blades on a wheel and causing it to spin. A wind turbine helps create renewable energy.

voltage (VOHL-tij): Voltage is an electrical force that is expressed in volts. Electricians have to work with high voltage.

TO LEARN MORE

BOOKS

Graham, Ian. *You Wouldn't Want to Live Without Electricity!* New York, NY: Franklin Watts, 2015.

Nydal Dahl, Øyvind. *Electronics for Kids.* San Francisco, CA: No Starch Press, 2016.

Parker, Steve. *Electricity.* New York, NY: DK, 2013.

WEBSITES

Visit our website for links about electricity: **childsworld.com/links**

Note to Parents, Teachers, and Librarians: We routinely verify our Web links to make sure they are safe and active sites. So encourage your readers to check them out!

SELECTED BIBLIOGRAPHY

"Electrical." *United States Department of Labor*, n.d., osha.gov. Accessed 13 Mar. 2019.

"Electricians." *Bureau of Labor Statistics*, n.d., bls.gov. Accessed 13 Mar. 2019.

"Everything You Need to Know about Wind Turbine Technicians." *Energy*, n.d., energy.gov. Accessed 13 Mar. 2019.

INDEX

ABOUT THE AUTHOR

Heidi Ayarbe is an author, storyteller, and translator. She grew up in Nevada and has lived and traveled all over the world.